Summer's Drowning

Copyright © 2014 by Greg Schaffer

All rights reserved

No part of this book may be reproduced in any form or by any electronic or mechanical means including information storage and retrieval systems, without permission in writing from the author. The only exception is by a reviewer, who may quote short excerpts in a review.

This is a work of fiction. Names, characters, businesses, places, events and incidents are either the products of the author's imagination or used in a fictitious manner. Any resemblance to actual persons, living or dead, or actual events is purely coincidental.

ISBN 978-0-9911052-2-9 (paperback)

ISBN 978-0-9911052-3-6 (ebook)

www.facebook.com/summersdrowning

Second Chance Publishing
www.secondchancebook.org

Contents

BEFORE 1
    Fish on a Bike 3
    Buffalo Blues 5
    Friends First 7
    Just Two Friends 9
    Where Are You Tonight? 11
    Past and Present 13
    What Do You Want? 15
    A Midwinter's Night Dream 17
    Awakenings 19

DURING 21
    Brought Us Together 23
    I'm Here 25
    The Veteran 27
    The Greatest Gift 29
    The Time is at Hand 31
    It's About Love 35
    First Love Poem 37
    Survivors Second 39
    It's Our Show 41

FALLING APART 43
    Did You Really Mean? 45
    Listen Now 47

Don't 49

Soul Mate or Checkmate? 51

Resistance Can Bind 53

Not My Lasagna 55

I 57

AFTER 59

Me, You, No 61

And So It Ends 63

Cold Reality 65

Seeds 67

Trails 69

Never Ending 71

Summer's Drowning 73

There 77

Past 79

Steel Walls 81

HOPE 83

Good Mourning 85

Boulevard of Broken Dreams 87

Lucky Man 89

Winds of Soul 91

Shells of Love 93

Perhaps 95

Beget 97

Hope 99

BEFORE

Fish on a Bike

She was all I had seen
Once a long time ago in a dream
That I turned away

Tomorrow on a lonely night
I gave in to the fight
Of what might have been

Oh, a fish on a bike
The one I never loved
Never even knew if I liked
She left, the fish on a bike

Sitting on a hard bar stool
People telling me I was a fool
What do they know?

Cheap crap played out every day
On soaps or on Springer in some ugly way
Love really blows

Roly poly, holy moly!
What's the one thing to console me
Besides an empty beer

Loneliness is here again
Because I've gave in to the sin
To the fear

Oh, a fish on a bike
The one I never loved
Never even knew if I liked
She left, the fish on a bike

Buffalo Blues

She was so fine
I nearly lost my mind
But she cut her losses dry
And behind herself she cried
She was wondering the town
Because Bethlehem was down
And she cried

    She's got the Buffalo Blues
    She's got nothing left to lose

Her friends are getting married
Her life is so harried
But she makes each day a dream
By saying what she means
Yet she still takes her licks
And never gets her kicks
Still she cries

    She's got the Buffalo Blues
    She's got nothing more to choose

Friends First

We met in a time, we touched our lives
Too many problems that we both had to hide
We needed someone, someone to take our hand
For the moment, someone who would understand

Time continued on, and we became close quite fast
Sometimes wondering if our friendship will last
Complicated by feelings that we didn't understand
Why can't we take that one step back?
Why do we fear some attack?
When all I did was take your hand

Friends first, please understand
Friends first, it's all that's at hand
Don't think too hard about what can be
Try to discover the friend that's me
Friends first, please understand

There will be times, when you want to cry out
Feelings of hurt that you just can't sort out
Don't be afraid to call me, I am there for you
A shoulder and an ear is all that I can do

Maybe one day, we will someday fall in love
But until that time, there is something to resolve
There is no pressure, no rushing, no expectations
I am not here to create more complications

Friends first, is what I need now
Friends first, to get over the pain somehow
I want you to be sure of this
I want to be a friend on your list
Friends first, later we'll worry about tomorrow

And if we find that we're destined to simply be friends
Then that's only the beginning, not the end
In this world of hurt and uncaring there is not enough
Of those who truly care to help when times are tough

And I want you to know,
Wherever you may go
I am always first, and foremost,
Your friend...
...to the end.

Just Two Friends

There's a light in your eyes that I've seen before
That oh so often seems to lead to more
But broken hearts and wasted times
Seem to always deny what I thought was mine

This has hardened this man's soul
It took away all of my control
Don't get me wrong, as I'm not opposed
I'm just no longer the type to impose

I'm not the hunter, you're not the prey
We're just two friends who met along the way

But I've seen it before and I'm sick and tired
Of seeing it blown when I was inspired
Perhaps singularity is simply my was
If that's my destiny well then that's ok

I know that you've been hurt like me
But I don't know exactly what you see
I'm not someone you should turn away
First and foremost I'm your friend today

I'm not the fire and you're not the flame
We're just two friends who were burned along the way

No one knows if we have the courage
To throw away our personal baggage
But to you and me that does not matter
Because within friendship such barriers shatter

So at times I still glance into your eyes
I never considered you a possible prize
But on a level I've always ignored
I feel your presence and I am consoled

I'm not the hunter, you're not the prey
We're just two friends who met along the way

Is it possible that a woman and a man
Can ignore the bullshit and then understand?
But I'm not the hunter and you're not the pray
We've always been two friends who met along the way

Where Are You Tonight?

Where are you tonight?
Are you feeling all right?
What did you have for breakfast today?
What kind of words did you say?
I need to know
What are you feeling like?
Oh, I need to know
My soul mate
Where are you tonight?

What is your life like?
Are you full of happiness or of spite?
Are you living alone or in some other way?
Where do you go to work every day?
I need to know
Will you love me too?
Have we ever met?
My soul mate
Where are you tonight?

I just want you to know
That I need you too
And I want to stop looking
Because I know it's true
Somewhere
Somewhere
Somewhere

Past and Present

Events of past and events of present
Came crashing in a single swirl
Ages of idle for a precious moment
With one special girl

Not seen – invisible
A force that stands above
Not material – intangible
Yet real, it's love

Stupid yes – stupid no
Only as stupid as you say so
I want you – you'll only go
Life's too short – you have to know

You were warm but I was cool
You wanted me – I wanted you too
I became scared – I turned from you
You became frustrated – I was a damn fool

Will you listen? Will you hear?
The desperate sounds of my dreams
I think of you, I wipe away a tear
This ain't right – it can't be as it seems

What Do You Want?

Here I sit
And dream about
A face I've known
So many times

I don't know why
I even care
But why does she
Always dare?

What do you want?
Tell me now
What do you want
From me?

But what do you want
I have to know
What can I do
For you?

I have so much
To give to you
We can go so far
But where to?

Tell me now
What can I give you
All I want
Is to have you

What do you want?
Do I have it?
What do you want
From me?

A Midwinter's Night Dream

We've known each other for quite some time
It's been much longer than a year
We slowly became friends
But, as it is with all trends
This soon began to disappear

No, not on the outside, no one could see
I'm the sole one to blame
You like me, sure, I know
But "as friends" is as far as you'll go
I'm sorry, I don't think I feel the same

Like all love stories and soap operas
I long to be with you, arm in arm
Sometimes I'd think for awhile
And I'd end up with a smile
'Cause you make me feel so warm

Then I'd snap out of those dreams
Those dreamt a thousand times
By a thousand people before
I think for awhile; it seems
To fit with some awful crimes
To love a friend who wants no more

Of course I really don't know that
But I'm pretty good at assuming
I'm scared of rejection
I need someone's protection
I'm afraid you'll be uncaring

So, you see my dilemma
It's a problem I've got to solve
I want your understanding
I need your caring
But most of all, I want your love

Awakenings

Frozen from the journey through the tundra
I find myself crawling out from under
Frost bitten toes, a runny nose
Glazed over eyes, frozen cries
Staring at the rising sun

Stumbling across the whitened ground
Exhausted from this journey I've found
Lost in my way, willing to pay
With a faith in God and a silent nod
Making my way to the welcoming town

Asleep for all this time
Enchanted by the dreams in my mind
Staunchly alone not giving up that solitude
That perseveres throughout my manhood

She touched my hand and opened my soul
An ear to listen and a heart to console
That night saw me weep so much
At the realization of that touch
For I was reminded that life isn't always cold

In that short instant she brought out from within
The hope that somewhere, sometime I could begin
Perhaps not here, perhaps not now
But simply to realize that I still knew how
Was perhaps the greatest gift from a friend

So to you who has strolled into my life
And without knowing has helped me face my strife
I am glad for the awakening
To come in from the cold that I've been faking

And though we may be no more than friends
It is that gift that you unknowingly gave me that I'll take to the end

Thank you, it was cold

DURING

Brought Us Together

You were young, and I was old
It wouldn't work, that's what we were told
It would need a little luck
If we could turn our love around and make it work

I knew it would always be
Us here together, together forever
Before I couldn't see
The love you always knew would bring us together

We were friends, that's all I thought
I never knew that it would lead to this
But then it happened, the love you sought
From me emerged when we first kissed

Now I see it clear
And I will always be here
And the good times
And the bad times
We'll face together and make it through

The argument we had back then
Just doesn't seem to matter anymore
We fought and cried
The tears we dried
And came together hand in hand

It brought us together
Us here together, together forever
Before I couldn't see
The faith you had that we would be together

I'm Here

You were there, you were crying
But when I arrived you were gone
You are hurt, there's no denying
No matter what you think, you're not alone

Across the miles I can feel
What it is doing to you
Your suffering is so bad, so real
I want to help, I want to feel it, too

I'm away from you, so damn powerless
Someone I love is in despair
And here I am, oh so far away
This feeling of helplessness
Settles over me; it's in the air
Is there anything I can do or say?

When I needed you, you were there
Now I'm here for you, and the hurt we'll share

Let me bear your fears
Let me carry your load
Here's my shoulder, cry, cry
Let it out, let go the tears
Don't act secure, don't act bold
I want to help, let me try

When I needed you, you were there
Now I'm here for you, and the hurt we'll share

I know a piece of you has been ripped
A part of your life is gone
You feel knocked down, punched and kicked
But life continues, life goes on

I want to share your burden
I want to share your load
Please let me come in
It hurts me to see you hurt so

When I needed you, you were there
Now I'm here for you, and the hurt we'll share

Well, maybe you're thinking it's all dead
But I'll be here to help you
And you'll see the beautiful times ahead
Life can be bad, but it can be good, too

The Veteran

You see me, and I see you
And I see me, inside of you
We turned and faced our eyes
And saw the mating of our lives
You cried and I cried, too

The sins of society upon us
The thinking of people so unjust
They laugh and point and stare
All we can do is wonder where
Where are people who see more than lust

I love you, you love me
And we both know, we can never be
Not here, not now, perhaps sometime
I will be yours, and you will be mine

I mumble and stare into my drink
I recall that I used to love to think
But now all I think of is love
I'm at much at peace as a chained dove
I've fallen so fast, I fear I'll sink

You see another
I sit and wonder
Is that what you want
Or is that what must be
Must we never say the forbidden word "we"

As time goes on, our lives are separate
Those dreams are beginning to look desperate
But we meet again, and the time is right
We share a day, we share a night
We realize that our needs were never met

I see you, and you see me
The courage is gained, utter the word "we"
We are together as we should
Our lives are one, they never could
Be separate again, my sweet beauty

The Greatest Gift

It was a truth I had learned to accept
They all say you never feel love in the same respect
Once it is torn from your soul
I knew I was destined to simply settle
To never again reach that level
Of true love, complete and total

You touched my hand and brought it all back
You reached for me and instinctively I began to react
You showed me how to feel
That is the greatest gift of all
To know that I have the ability to again fall
To again know that love is real

You didn't do anything
But be your caring self
You didn't say anything
You were only your caring self

I do not know if this will last
Or if these feelings of love will fade into the past
None of that matters as much right now
Can you see just what you have given to my being?
Can you understand what it is that I have been seeing?
In your eyes, the spark to love I have found

Resuscitation of the innermost fears have not occurred
Respiration of the amorous lungs has preserved
Restoration of the vision removes sites blurred
Revelation of the gift has left me assured

You touched my hand and brought it all back
You reached for me and instinctively I began to react
You showed me love so strong
That is the greatest gift of all
To know that I have the ability to again fall
To know that to love is not wrong

You may stay, you may go, no one can tell
But there are no other visions that you need sell
You have given me the greatest gift of all
I know I can love now fully from the soul

The Time is at Hand

Two steps forward, one step back
It's hard to throw this monkey from my back
Across the ice I slip and slide
At night I swim against the tide
My life seems to lead to some awful cul-de-sac

Between third and home, caught in a pickoff
The damned race is one giant ripoff
What a joke of a situation
What a blow to my reputation
I seek the future in a bottle of Smirnoff

Pressure's on, the time is at hand
Hold fast, gotta make my stand
Haunting past, never far from my soul
Release the chains, the time is at hand

The pain of so much effort stabs at me
All I did now rots at the bottom of the sea
They build the park as a sanctuary
The machines push the dirt so arbitrarily
With no cares to create condos of mediocrity

The bile swells up as testament to the bitterness
Of existing in all of this manufactured uselessness
But now I stray, and can't seem to find the path
Worried today's actions will be tomorrow's aftermath
Blind to beauty, cursing the damn sightlessness

Pressure's on, the time is at hand
Praying that somehow she'll understand
Bitterness and loneliness is not my goal
Chisel at the wall, the time is at hand

Oh, how can I ever regain the innocence?
This self-imposed prison just doesn't make sense
I want to go ahead, but I feel tied to my fate
She may be the key to opening the gate
If she will only see through this evil pretense

She takes my hand and we walk together
The burden on my back feels lighter than a feather
Her warmth and passion melts the slippery ice
She provides the rescue from the liquid's vice
She shines a light to lead us out of the weather

Pressure builds, the time is at hand
But at night I wonder if she really understands
I know my past has certainly taken its' toll
I wonder if I'm ready for the time at hand

And if it seems that I may be a bit confused
Don't worry if I'm quiet and bemused
I must plan thoroughly if I am to learn from the past
Like the grand pyramids, the next time will last
I am damn tired of my soul being abused

So I realize that I must face this time that I'm in
And I try to put to bed the intense pain so I can begin
I close the self-loathing chapter this time
Church bells rings and I hear the chime
The pain I feel is another's sin

The pressure eases, the time is at hand
Feet planted firmly, ready to make that stand
Before will always be a part of my soul
But the chains are breaking at the time at hand

The pressure eases, the time is at hand
At least a part I know she tries to understand
Happiness and togetherness is my goal
Great walls fall when the time is at hand

Pressure subsides, the time is at hand
Uncertainty eases when she says she understands
The road is long but I've paid the toll
Ready or not, the time is at hand

Release the pressure, the time is at hand
Save my soul, the time is at hand
Break the chains, the time is at hand
Build the bridge, the time is at hand
Take my hand, the time is at hand
Hold my body, the time is at hand
Knock down the wall, the time is at hand
Listen to me, the time is at hand
Run with me, the time is at hand

It's About Love

Seeing you there is all I need
To convince me just to believe
There's no one else I could ever want
There's no one else I can think about
It's just you

It's about love
Love
Love

Lying next to me in bed
Almost can't believe the words you said
When I said, "I think that I love you"
You said, "I know, I feel it too"
Then I knew

It's about love
Love
Love

Walking down the street at night
I can feel your hand holding me tight
And I cling on to that possibility
That you're becoming a part of my reality
Can it be true?

It's about love
Love
Love

First Love Poem

I lay awake in my bed
The clock reads an unmerciful 3 AM
I think of her, and what she said
And I smile

We met as friends, nothing more
She was nice but I was taken
I really wasn't planning to score
But I smiled

Well, one day we talked like never before
I realized that I'd never known her
She's sweet and kind, not a bore
And she smiled

We sat alone and talked
And laughed, and cried, as old friends
And new lovers – a line was crossed
The line so thin that never ends
That can separate two from being one
That can prevent some from seeing the sun

I remember when we first kissed
It was that dance on Valentine's Day
I saw a chance – it wouldn't be missed
And we smiled

I feel as if I'm floating
I know that it is true
Hey, I'm really not much for quoting
But I remember you said, "I love you"

I'm drifting in a haze of beauty
Of colors of yellow, green, and blue
I guess all I really wanted to say
Is I love you, truly, too

Survivors Second

We shared our thoughts, we let down our fears
We shared our problems, we shared our tears
You took my hand, and I took yours
Exposing our pains we fought to ignore

Time was our ally, the friendship blossomed
To something neither of us was accustomed
Our feelings we soon began to understand
We realized we could step forward
We had the courage to move toward
That safe haven of our own private island

Survivors second, there is hope of a tomorrow
Survivors second, there is love after sorrow
If you look hard you may see
There's a future out there with me
Survivors second, we made it to tomorrow

Those crying times, when we were alone
When feelings of hurt turned our hearts to stone
I lost my fear and reached out to you
I wanted to show you all I could do

The day has come when we knew we were in love
The hurts of the past we had the strength to resolve
Strength born of trust, we shout "I've survived!"
Together relishing the warmth of being alive

Survivors second, we've made it this far
Survivors second, sick of playing the martyr
We were friends first, but now we've grown
Together as survivors of circumstances we own
Survivors second, now we can touch that star

And along the line we knew we were more than friends
The love that we felt we simply could no longer pretend
You have shown me there really is love in the world
We've survived better than we thought we ever could

And remember that I need you
And I am always thinking of you
And of us, and of tomorrows
Together…
…we have managed to survive.

It's Our Show

Here we are, trying to make a dream come true
Trying to make a life with you
Is just what I'm trying to do

There you sit, trying to do the best you can
Trying in earnest to remember when
We laid the first bricks with our hands

So we sit, scared like little children
And pray to God
For that someday when
We can be proud

There they walk, angry because we're growing up
Not having themselves made that jump
Looking but too blind to see

Where, they say, are you going to realize your dreams
It isn't as easy as it may seem
Yes, it's not easy to do
But I go, led on my a light of faith
Searching for that place where I may feel safe
Knowing it lies within you

Still they scream that we don't know it all
Worrying that we're gonna fall
I'll tell them all
That if we crash we'll still stand tall

Here we go, living our lives the best we can
Yearning so hard to understand
That our futures lie within our hearts

So they can go and talk to their heart's content
Looking for problems they think they can prevent
We know they'll never find any

We are doing what we want to do
I can back out if I wanted to
But why would I go
You know by now
I'm not losing you

So there you go, walking down the aisle in white
Making such a beautiful sight
And there I am, trying to maintain a rigid stand
Sweat trickles on the palm of my hand
About to marry my best friend

We are the stars
Of our own show

FALLING APART

Did You Really Mean?

Standing here, in the gateway
Standing holding my own
Misunderstanding and a preconception
No one told me that it was wrong
But I can't read your mind
Can you stop and spend some time?

Somehow I thought I knew the story
Somehow I was wrong
The only thing that really was missing
Was a friend in you that I thought was gone
Whatever got in the way?
How did we let it slip away?

Did you really mean the things that you said?
Did you really mean to throw it all away?

I don't believe it's gone forever
I don't believe it at all
Something in the way you looked
Told me that there's more behind the wall
Will you break it down?
Or will you help break down mine?

Suddenly I see another side
Suddenly I see more
A glimpse of what might have happened
Showed me what I was fighting for
But I can't read your mind
Can you stop and spare some time?

Did you really mean the things that you said?
Did you really mean to throw it all away?

Standing here, in the gateway
Standing holding my own
Misunderstanding and a preconception
No one told me that I was wrong
But I can't read your mind
Can you stop and spend some time?

Listen Now

You say you're being ignored
You say you're feeling kind of bored
Too many times this has happened to you
Too many ways you felt you were screwed

I don't understand the last page
I can't see what inspired your rage
Too many times of searching for a soul mate
Has twisted my heart into images of hate

Listen now, it isn't all over
Listen now don't think it's all over
Stand your ground and continue to listen
I know your past but continue to listen
Listen now

This is not the way that we were
This is not of that I feel sure
But I don't want to say no
But I don't want to go

Listen now, it isn't all over
Listen now don't think it's all over
Stand your ground and continue to listen
I know your past but continue to listen
Listen now

Don't

Don't say maybe
Don't say you'll try
Don't say another time
Don't say why
Don't say goodbye
Don't leave
Don't hate me
Don't turn away

Soul Mate or Checkmate?

You woke up yesterday
Laid your head down and prayed
That something different would come of this

I remember my mistakes
Saw how much your heart aches
But I still carry this fight inside

You see, I don't mean to play games
I'm not in it for wasting time
Or to claim something as mine
Perhaps it's really me to blame
I really need to know
Is it soul mate or checkmate?

Is it soul mate or checkmate?
Is it forever or a trap?
Is it simply fate or is it too late
To go forward or to go back

I came home from the steel mill
You were awake and strong willed
Had to prove that you were right

I turned around and headed out
Had to go and figure out
Why I carry this fight inside

I came back late yesterday
You had packed and went away
No call, no note, no chance

You said you tried to show it to me
I faltered so you said it was not meant to be
That chance is now a thing of the past

Is it soul mate or checkmate?
Is it forever or a trap?
Is it simply fate or is it too late
To go forward or to go back

I woke up alone today
Kneeled by my bed and prayed
That one day I'd have the courage to decide

Resistance Can Bind

No more reason to believe
Forced her to leave
That was her only choice

Too many times in the past
She'd tried to make it last
She'd ignore her friend's noise

You don't realize the cost
Until you realize it's lost
And you're not yourself

They had all tried to tell you
That he'd simply use you
And think only of himself

So now you find
You're not feeling all alone
There's still another home
Resistance can bind
Until you see what is right
Then the target is in sight and you can fight

They say love is blind
Only when the hurt's behind
Is when you can see

But futility of resistance
To deny that coexistence
Is all you need

Resist the urge
To forget about the bad
Don't dwell on the sad
Resistance is good
It can help to make you strong
You're not alone and you were never wrong

You don't realize the cost
Until you realize it's lost
And you're not yourself

But it is time to return
To the status you have earned
To tell that ass to kiss off

Not My Lasagna

I knew we had issues
When I asked you where you'd been
It ended with tears in tissues
And silence not so golden

After the argument was done
I tried hard to believe
Off at ten, home at one
Wasn't a method to deceive

The next day I was late
Work of the day was long
Did you have a dinner date?
What I saw was too wrong

I opened the refrigerator
It was not my lasagna
What was it doing there
These layers of pasta?
Years of past it was our tradition
This lasagna was not our creation

I didn't want to admit it
I didn't want to stay
It would be the same old script
No matter what you'd say

You I never wanted to be without
Leaving took everything I had
When I returned, you were out
I opened the fridge to see what you had

When I looked inside
It was not my lasagna
I ignored my pride
And ate of the pasta
Years of past it was our tradition
This lasagna was not our creation

Layers of pasta and cheese
Melting throughout the pan
No amount of season
Can spice it up again
Years of past it was our tradition
This lasagna was not our creation

I

I want to say goodbye
I want to end it now

AFTER

Me, You, No

One's away
One's to stay...no more

Too many times I have tried
Too many times I have failed
To many times the answer is...no

Neither you without me
Nor me without you
No more

And So It Ends

And so it ends
There is no more left to do
And so it ends
There's no more I must prove

Certainly after years of life
I can say it was worth the sacrifice

I need to know
That what I miss
Is not a person from long ago
Is not a life of bliss

A time turned bleak
A life that I mourn
And not a person I seek
So let me go on

The pain and the hurt
Is all I can feel
Crying, because I know it's real

Cold Reality

So here I am
The ugliness of it all over my head
Feeling close to dead

This cold reality
Has left me with every ounce of proof
To recognize the hard truth

It's over
All that we had is gone
It's over
Tell me who has won?

The clock on the wall
Is ticking I am aware
Counting off the time we'll never share

In my heart
I can still feel it all
But I know it's only a shadow in the wall

To laugh with you
Is all that I really wish
And I hate to see it end like this

Seeds

I walked along the shore alone
Away from the mirage that I thought was home
Feeling tense and feeling wrong
Struggling just to remain strong

My care for you words couldn't express
Seeing you go is my worst regret
Thinking you killed this romance
We deserved one more chance

You need to find your own way
There's nothing else that I can say
So now I have to jump aside
Praying you will realize

Seeds you plant and help them grow
Seeds you need to reap and sow
Nothing happens overnight
Nothing grows if you deny the light
To your seeds

Swimming in the consequence
Of this lonely circumstance
Fighting not to reminisce
About the future that I missed

With sorrow I released the rigging
One who never thought of begging
Now the winds will push me away
With only these words left to say

Seeds you plant and help them grow
Seeds you need to reap and sow
Nothing happens overnight
Nothing grows if you deny the light
To your seeds

The rhetoric invades my head
Psychologically I wish I was dead
The only thing that kills inside
Is seeing all those seeds that died

All you had to do was wait
The planted seeds needed time to take
But time was a luxury denied
The exposed seeds withered and died

Seeds you plant and help them grow
Seeds you need to reap and sow
Nothing happens overnight
Nothing grows if you deny the light
To your seeds

Trails

Hell, I don't know what's wrong or right
Deep down within I live this perpetual fight
Two times beaten, not going down for a third
Always knowing I have to have the last word
Entrapped from within, afraid of the night

The lyrics speak of battles once raged
Of the conflicts with such ferocity I engaged
Turn to the left, get stabbed in the back
Ever looking out for another attack
Learning to avoid wondering if I should have stayed

One who laughs, one who cries
One who lives, one who dies
One who always needs to see proof
One who's afraid of the blatant truth

I walk alone this virgin trail
Tempted by evils that lead men to hell
I can't give in, but I can't look behind
Too deaf to hear words, too blind to see signs
Alone, I seek answers to no avail

Bitterness still rages after all these years
Too tired to stop, afraid of facing fears
Our bed lies in ruin, our life together gone
Separate trails we embarked on
Alone on the trail as it appears

Blazing this trail, I see yesterday's horrors
Bound by rage, hiding from the hours
No one seems to know, no one cares
No one can understand the monumental errors
Trail blazers or merely cowards?

Never Ending

Cold stare, glass look
Strange unfriendly morning
One glance was all it took
A long way to go
A bad feeling to know
Once a glare, now rapidly dimming

Sad face, sweet tear
I should have left it
She's here – so near
I would have gone
But she kept me on
Though the shoe did not fit

Why is it always me
Why can't I see
What is wrong or right
Oh, she's so tempting
But it's all never ending
I've got no strength left to fight

Warm touch, tender kiss
I sure miss those days
Hating face, clenched fist
Screaming unpleasant obscenities
Smashing all of my fantasies
I guess these are now the ways

It happened way too soon
Like an endless desert dune
It's not really going to change
If I remain as is
I'll only score a miss
And things will remain the same

So I sit here
In my own little world
That I find so unreal and weird
They wonder why
I stare and cry
As I wipe away each tear

It's never ending

Summer's Drowning

So at times I still take to the streets
Lost in the darkness of years gone by
So maybe it's you I'm hoping to see
And recapture a bit of what made me smile

Those were the times that were lost forever
Drowned in the lake of the lost souls
There was no more time to remember
All the pain that time does allow

If there was a chance I'd try to take it
So innocent yet burned at the state
Allowing nothing to consummate
The lands of endless heartbreak

I tried hard just to let you go
I finally did it (summer's drowning)
Never looked back after checking the rear view
A hundred times (summer's drowning)
Why say there's a chance if you can't back it
With a shred of truth (summer's drowning)
If you meant it you'd forget the lies
And just state your mind (summer's drowning)

And so you come to me now
And I try some how
To shut you off from what I want
Drowning in a summer's sorrow
With no hope of another tomorrow
Forcing me to shun what I really want

Summer's drowning

I forgot about you when I said goodbye
Began my new life so many miles away
My growth was endless when I let my soul fly
Without the chains of giving you your way

You called me once to make amends
I wondered how I could settle for that
Bit my lip and said let's just be friends
Playing my feelings like Russian Roulette

But for now I wish I had acted differently
For one more chance (summer's drowning)
After seeing you there with "Captain Jack"
In the background (summer's drowning)
I gave in to rumors and to the past
Unbelievable circumstance (summer's drowning)
Met with looks of betrayal and confusion
Buried in the ground (summer's drowning)

Take a photograph
Memories make me laugh
But it's all gone despite the sorrow
It was the most beautiful experience
It still hurts to reminisce
All gone thanks to summer's drowning

Summer's drowning

June was forever and always
July saw war and fighting
August came and commitment was gone
September ended always

I can't say there was nothing
But I have to hate it all
But how can I with all the love that I saw?

Summer's drowning

So now I accept my path of life
And I know it was lost long ago
Why does a fool relive the strife?
Does a fool know just when to let go?

And while I can't understand the distance
Between souls that once were mates
I can only accept this chosen silence
And simply stare at closed, rusted gates

It was hard to let you go
But I finally did it (summer's drowning)
Never looked back after checking the rear view
A hundred times (summer's drowning)
I know it's forever gone
The friend in you (summer's drowning)
Despite my fight it will always be
Separate lives (summer's drowning)

And I miss your company
And I miss your time
And I miss your friendship
And your hand in mine

There

There
I would stand, I would stay
And I would go, and I would lie
And I would get up and try
There

There
You would lay, you would turn
And you would say, and you would lie
And you would give in and cry
There

There
We would play, we would laugh
And we would want, and we would fly
And we would bind then unwind
There

There
We never really cared
We never really shared
We were only
There

There
I'm alone, I am gray
I have no home, my place is wrong
The past is gone I don't belong
There

Past

And so, I sit and reject
And so, I try to project
A reason, a rationale of where the time went

And so, I cannot understand
Why that reason is not at hand
For one thing is that I refuse to bend

Those times I fight hard to remember
Most of which I cannot surrender
The life of the past that never would last

No matter how hard that I try
The echoes constitute a subliminal lie
Of a life that is gone and I no longer belong

So maybe it's only a glimpse
Of a past experience
That I try to recapture
In doing so do I deny
The present in my eyes
By not closing these chapters?

So as hard as I try I cannot realize
That which was here before
And as far as I go to the land of the snow
Pulled by the past's lore

As long as I continue to live
In the dark reaches of the mind
I cannot even let myself give
The gift of the proper time

And I find myself in the past
Looking for glory days I want to last

Steel Walls

In the city there can stand no one
Who can say what remains is what's won
The challenges they face day-to-day
Circle above to remind of the way
Of when the days were warm

A steel wall encases my heart
Constructed the day we moved apart
Fortress against invaders external
A cage to keep what's left internal
A shadow of your memory within

The cold December sun lights the darkness
But only for a while before consumed by loneliness
All streets lead to temptation
Giving in yields more frustration
Not the light that I try to harness

Today is late and that time has since past
And in only my dreams can I make it last
Foolish yearnings for what you don't need
Can't wash it away, forever it will bleed
Fortify the steel walls is all I can ask

And within these walls I shall die
Always wondering if you too still cry

HOPE

Good Mourning

Lord, give me the wisdom to know
What I mourn is not a person,
But a life I once had, and
Lord, give me the strength
To let it go…
So that today I may live.

Boulevard of Broken Dreams

We all make our choices
As hard as they may seem
And sometimes we end up walking
Down the Boulevard of Broken Dreams

I sit at the end of the Phillies Café
I slowly drink my coffee the James Dean way
And in the cracked mirror I can see
That ghostly image of what was once me
Knowing this is a tab that I must pay

For that one chance I had to take
To determine what was real and what was fake
With it I couldn't go any farther
Unless I became a selfish martyr
Knowing that the sacrifice was somehow a mistake

My feet are swollen, the blisters red
The rain on the street makes the asphalt gleam
Not quite sure what I could have done instead
To avoid this Boulevard of Broken Dreams

Down the Boulevard, it's a long haul
Across the Boulevard is a lonely pool hall
For the dreams are broken, the souls have died
A haven, a refuge for those who tried

At the café I will never share this meal
Never share with you that which I feel
For our tomorrows became yesterdays
And we went our own separate ways
The Boulevard now has become too real

I tell you this so you will know
That everything happened as you said it'd go
You knew, I knew but I had to try
Trashing those chains, I can now reach the sky
But I must still ramble down the Boulevard so slow

And if one day you're walking by
The Boulevard where grown men can cry
Stop by Phillies and order Cappuccino
For then together we can go
And leave the Boulevard to touch the sky

Lucky Man

The air outside was cold
My face was red and burning
It's bad, or so I'm told
But my heart is warm and learning
I guess I really wanted to see
Why you keep returning
It's the same old story all over again
I've got to realize I'm a lucky man

I look way over across the bar
And I see her smiling
Well, it wouldn't go too far
And my heart is just pretending
I think of talking to her
To find out what she's giving
Then I sit and remember when
I know you love me and I'm a lucky man

It's the same thing all of the time
I'm yours and you are mine
But sometimes I still remember when
We were so hurting
You came around and you took my hand
I began to think I'm a lucky man

Here I am, so far away
From your loving arms
I never knew what to say
When your kisses set off my alarms
I've got to somehow let you know
I'm not going to demand
I want to take you by the hand
And let you know I'm a lucky man

So do you lie awake in bed
And wonder what I'm doing
At those times just remember when
Your touch kept my heart turning
We can never make it through this
Unless we keep learning
Till then I'll sit back and pretend
That all is cool and I'm a lucky man

God knows love makes a man a fool
It reaches in and takes its cool
But somehow so long ago
All of my luck ran out
Alone and scarred is how I now stand
A shell of what was once a lucky man

If you can still give then I'll receive
And we can start all over again
Just give me a reason and I'll believe
Your love still exists in the end
But for now I'll just lick my wounds
And remember I was once a lucky man

Winds of Soul

I never knew I would outlive the past
Our friendship had fallen out of my grasp
I never wanted that to end
I still wanted to be your friend
Like it was in the past
I thought that would last

But it's good to see
That you're doing fine
And that I can say
After all this time
I'm glad you're still a friend of mine

Listen there, the winds of your soul
Are whispering the words you already know
You are as curious as me
Inside you want to see
Where did that closeness go?
You need to know

I don't want to go back
I don't want to reverse
I could never return to that relationship cursed
But above all of the problems
And the badness that we shared
Between us our friendship was blessed

So now I know for sure
That you are truly secure
And happy in your life
Safe from any serious strife
Living life as happy as you can
I understand

Well I don't want to forget
I don't want to deny
I don't want to forget that past of mine
But today I tell you
I'm glad you took that step
And that my hand of friendship you did accept

Here I am, what the die had cast
Trying to shake that ghost from my past
Wanting to know you're ok
Just to break down the wall in our way
Knowing that it can't last
It's in the past

But it's good to see
That you're doing fine
When all the love and hate have drained
I always knew the friendship remained
I'm glad you're doing fine

Shells of Love

Last night, as I lay in my bed and dreamt
Images of you played within, in some imaginary event
Time had passed too long for us to regain
You were secure in your life, despite the pain
You shook your head, turned away, our love was spent

I woke up this morning in a wave of nausea
Crying inside, pulsating with nostalgia
I remembered how much I cherished her touch
To know I'd never hold her again was just too much
It wasn't her I missed, only the outward shell of love

Shells of love are all that there is
Rings on a tree mark the time of existence
We all try to remain
We all want the same
Walking on these shells of love

Hard to recall the bad, easy to see the good
Sometimes I get selective amnesia, though I understood
In every relationship there is the outside and the inside
The inside is what counts, appearance is for the outside
I miss the bark, forgetting the inside is rotted wood

As we walk along the shore of expansive experience
Each step carefully, slightly faster than total abstinence
Walking on eggshells, afraid that they'll crack
Not taking the practical lesson from the abstract
What's within defines, what's outside is a shell of love

Shells of love sometimes are all that remain
Some emotional skeleton that doesn't show past pain
We all try to walk
We all try to talk
We don't want to break these shells of love

I woke up this morning missing the times of yesterday
But I forgot those times made up the shell anyway
The inside is gone and no love is within the shell
It's hard to remember that much of it was hell
Shells last forever, relationships just fade away

Tomorrow I may find myself again trying to construct
Another shell of love with the supplies of the heart
But this time I'll concentrate on building the inside
To hell with appearance, we are side by side
Strengthening from within the shells of love

Shells of love are designed to protect
The love within, not to project
We fool ourselves often
We play with fire and burn
Let's strengthen these shells of love

Shells of love wash up on the shore
The animals who built them are no more
We regret emotional ties
And look into each other's eyes
And somehow find the power to build the shells of love

Perhaps

On a cold winter's day
In a place of no tomorrows
I saw it – someway
I saw happiness and sorrows

We left each other's arms
In a flash of flame
It was much to our alarms
Nothing would be the same

You left me, I left you
I tried, but what else could I do
You wanted him, I saw that again
Him as a lover, me as a friend

The weeks went by
The months separated us
I wondered how you could lie
I knew it was only lust

I forgot you – I found another
You forgot me – you knew some other
Our lives were separate – as separate as can be
You were you – I was I – we weren't we

Funny thing, it's called fate
With its' turns and twists
Not too soon, never too late
To meet again, from out of the mists

I saw you, sitting there
I admit I didn't recognize you
With your wild, sexy, new blond hair
I casually approached you

Suddenly, like a bolt of lightning
A flash of recognition entered my mind
Too late to escape, I turned to talking
To my surprise you weren't hostile, but kind

We talked and talked and talked again
About times past and present
I realized I had found an old friend
And perhaps…

Beget

Simply stated, it's a matter of proof
When we all try to discover the truth
Our souls are created with limitations
Unable to achieve measurable perfections
Torturing ourselves for human failings

There is no way I can ever discover
Elements lost that I'll never recover
Change is an inevitable occurrence
But no cause to react with petulance
Old seeds beget new seedlings

Forgive me, and set me free
Do it now and put your heart at ease
Let us forgive for that earlier time
So I can be yours and you can be mine

In the annals of history we find errors
Often largely founded in personal terrors

Hope

Still a wish, so far away
I held you here again today
The single thought racing through my mind
Is that we have lived through all the bad times

So perhaps after this long wait
The planted seeds really did take
I felt it when you touched my finger
In both of us those feelings linger

Seeds sprout up and always try
To reach high up to the sky
The winter's over, spring has returned
Shining light on what we have learned

From our seeds

www.ingramcontent.com/pod-product-compliance
Lightning Source LLC
Chambersburg PA
CBHW032045290426
44110CB00012B/958